FREE
THE
EAGLE

FREE
THE
EAGLE

Donald C. Kennedy

My grateful thanks to Floyd Suess
for his help and support.

Jacket design by Ken Miller

For my beloved Mary Kennedy
in Memorium

Contents

ROUND ONE

Troubled America

DESPITE the assurances of some of America's most reputable prognosticators, all is not well with America. Even though U.S. economic conditions have recently improved, don't think for a moment that all of America's economic problems have been solved.

Few nations have as many unemployed workers as does America. Today there are nearly 10 *million* unemployed in the U.S. Which should provide convincing proof that all is not well with our country.

Since 1970, the United States has had three economic recessions, which have left permanent scars on America. Those recessions have caused poverty and hardship for millions of Americans, and some of the damage persists to this day. Those recessions show that the U.S. economy lacks stability and strength.

Poverty is widespread in America today, and welfare and unemployment payments have seldom been so high. According to U.S. Government statistics, there are now *34 million* Americans living in poverty. That's one out of every seven Americans.

Why is this so, in incredibly rich America?

Few Americans know of the enormous effect of America's gigantic foreign trade deficits on the U.S. economy. Those deficits have been piling up since 1970 and now total more than *$250 billion.* In 1982 the U.S. merchandise deficit amounted to *$42.69 billion.* In 1983 it was *$65 billion.* Malcom Baldrige, Secretary of the U.S. Department of Commerce, predicts that the deficit for merchandise imports will jump to *$100 billion* in 1984. That's just for one year!

How can U.S. industry and employment prosper with foreign trade *merchandise deficits* of that size?

Visit any clothing store in your area. Examine the clothing labels. In most stores you'll find that at least half of the women's apparel comes from South Korea, China, Hong Kong, Sri Lanka, and the Philippines. In stores selling men's clothing it's the same story.

Not too long ago, apparel manufacture was a leading U.S. industry. It was even larger than the U.S. steel industry. But today that U.S. industry is in decline and employs fewer workers, nearly 400,000 fewer, than it did 20 years ago.

The U.S. apparel industry just can't match the low production costs in Third World countries. In Sri Lanka the average wage in the apparel industry is 19 cents an hour. In China it is $2 a day. Those are just a few examples. Obviously, the U.S. apparel industry can't meet that kind of competition.

In one year, 1982, the U.S. trade deficit in wearing apparel amounted to $7.7 billion.

Americans should know that America's apparel and textile industries cannot prosper unless imports are reduced. An unpleasant truth, but it's one that's plainly evident.

It's hard to believe, but now 65 percent of the shoes sold in the U.S. are imported. Most come from factories employing cheap labor in Third World countries. Largely because of this competition, more than 300 U.S. manufacturers of shoes have gone out of business since 1970. Some 100,000 American workers have lost their jobs as a result.

Since 1975, according to the U.S. Department of Labor, 13,000 industrial firms have failed in the United States. In one year, 1982, 3,000 U.S. industrial companies filed for bankruptcy. In California alone 560 industrial plants, employing 94,000 workers, closed in 1980. Some of this U.S. industrial disaster was unquestionably caused by foreign imports.

These have been rough times for U.S. industry and labor, and foreign imports are partly to blame.

During the last ten years, more than 3,000 U.S. manufacturers have moved to foreign locations to secure cheaper labor and operating costs, so as to compete with U.S. imports. Many were forced to do so to stay in business. Less industry and fewer jobs in the United States have resulted. How could it be otherwise?

Besides imports, American industry faces another serious problem. Many U.S. industrial plants need to be improved and modernized. In Japan the average industrial plant is nine years old. In the United States the average is 20 years.

It's been estimated that at least *$1.5 trillion* in investment money will be needed during the next few years to modernize U.S. industrial plants and build new ones. The question is, where will that enormous sum of investment money come from? Certainly it will not be available unless U.S. industry is profitable, and conditions encourage new industrial development. Which cannot be, if foreign imports continue to curtail U.S. industry.

The steel industry is another U.S. industry badly damaged by imports. During the last few years it has lost billions of dollars, and some predict that it will never regain its former size, or employ as many workers as it once did. Right now there are 200,000 fewer workers employed in the U.S. steel industry than there were just five years ago. Still, millions of tons of foreign steel are imported every year by the United States, and that takes away needed volume from U.S. mills. Does that make sense to you?

Recently the U.S. Steel Corporation, in an effort to reduce costs so as to compete with steel imports, dickered with the government-owned British Steel Company to import steel slabs from England. Other steel mills in the United States have also threatened to import unfinished steel from Brazil, Mexico and other low cost countries. If that should happen, more thousands of American steel workers will be without jobs. Many thousands of other workers in the U.S. coal and iron mining industries would also be affected. Does this make sense to you?

Steel is America's fourth largest industry and should not be lost because of imports.

At one time, the United States was the world's largest shipbuilder. Today less than 3 percent of the world's shipbuilding tonnage comes from American yards.

America's largest flag-line, SEA-LAND, INC., is now building a dozen 750-foot vanships in Japanese yards. Six other U.S. shipping companies are also building ships in Norwegian, South Korean, and Japanese yards. Not long ago the U.S. Maritime Commission approved the building of fourteen new container ships for U.S. LINES, to cost $780.5 million. Those ships are being built in South Korean yards.

Thirty years ago the United States had the largest fleet of merchant ships in the world. Now only 2½ percent of the world's ships fly the American flag. And only 4 percent of America's foreign commerce is carried in American ships.

In America, the manufacture of tires is no small industry. Forty-three factory plants now make tires in the U.S., and produce approximately 175 million tires annually. Now South Korea and Brazil are exporting tires to the U.S., and are offering them at reduced prices. I ask you: in what way do such imports benefit America?

Just inside Mexico's northern border are more than 300 American-owned industrial plants, all making products for export to the U.S. The average wage in many of those plants is $1 an hour. Is that fair to industries based in the U.S., that pay American wages, taxes, and other extra U.S. costs?

Imports have also affected the U.S. auto industry. Americans now buy more than two million foreign automobiles every year. Most are made by the Japanese, who now sell more cars in America than they do in their own country.

During the last few years, the U.S. auto industry has closed nearly 450 of its plants, and released one-third of its workers. In just one year, 1982, the U.S. foreign trade deficit in automobiles amounted to more than *$12 billion*. And those deficits continue.

It seems that the entire world wants to prosper at America's expense. And U.S. free trade has allowed them that advantage. As a result U.S. industry and employment have been badly damaged.

The U.S. should not import products that we can produce here in America. If we followed that rule the United States would have a more stable economy and America would be a more self-sufficient and prosperous nation.

ROUND TWO

Free Trade Examined

IT all began during the administration of President John F. Kennedy. It was he who sponsored, with Congressional approval, the present free trade policy of the United States government. That government measure was intended to aid in world economic development.

When President Kennedy initiated it, he removed or drastically cut U.S. tariffs and other controls that limited U.S. imports. He did so undoubtedly believing that other nations would follow America's leadership and example. Which they never did.

Other nations, to this day, have refused to abide by the free trade ideals advocated by the U.S. Government. They are more concerned about their own problems than those of their neighbors. With them, foreign trade is still trade and barter. Over the years they have learned that their own trading methods and customs are more practical and useful than some of the high-flying measures advocated by idealistic American politicians.

Since the time of President Kennedy, free trade has been the basic foreign trade policy of the U.S. Government. And the entire world has taken advantage of it. Because of it America has been flooded with imports from all over the world.

Look into any U.S. retail and wholesale store and see for yourself how foreign industry has taken over the U.S. marketplace. Which hasn't been good for America, or for the many thousands of U.S. workers who have lost their jobs because of it. Cheap imports have also caused more than 3,000 American firms to move their industrial operations to foreign lands, to reduce their production costs in order to market their products in the U.S.

America cannot afford free trade. Do you need more evidence to prove it?

Even Canada, our next-door-neighbor, isn't a disciple of free trade. For example, no outside industry can locate in Canada unless it promises to buy Canadian products and shows evidence that it will be of *significant benefit to Canada.* Applicants that can't meet those specifications are rejected. Canada's government policy is plainly *nationalistic.*

Japan also doesn't abide by the rules of free trade. Japanese government policy is resistant to imports, and because of it the Japanese domestic market is virtually closed to imports. Every possible measure is used to protect Japanese industry from import competition. The Japanese system is plainly *nationalistic,* and the Japanese have profited from it. Japan has become a world leader in trade and industry, and the Japanese economy is booming. And 98 percent of the Japanese people have jobs. Surely, Japan is doing something right!

Some people will tell you that we Americans should buy our needs from wherever they can be obtained at the lowest possible cost. Which means that we should buy them from China, Taiwan, Brazil, Mexico, Hong Kong, Singapore, the Philippines, and from other low-cost countries; rather than from our own U.S. industry.

That, my friend, is dangerous advice, for it means less industry for America, and fewer jobs for American workers. Also, in a long run, a lower standard of living for all Americans.

If that's what you want, that's what you'll get!

Today there are millions of workers without jobs in the U.S. Which is shameful, considering the enormous resources of America. Most of the jobless are unskilled workers. Many were formerly employed in hand-work and labor-intensive kinds of U.S. industry. Now much of that kind of industry is gone from America, closed out by low-cost imports. *And it's the American unskilled worker who has been hurt the most.*

America will always have a multitude of unskilled workers. And there should be jobs for them. And if it takes tariffs and import curbs to supply those jobs, then let's have them. Surely, that kind of U.S. industry, and those kinds of workers, should not be sacrificed on the altar of free trade.

Free trade can't be *fair trade* when so many countries have different labor and production costs. It's also an impossibility because so much foreign industry is government owned and subsidized. For example: today 40 percent of the world's copper, 33 percent of its iron, and 54 percent of world steel is produced by government owned or subsidized industry. Even 20 percent of world automobile production receives government support.

Even in agriculture, the United States has difficulty exporting its surplus farm products. Despite world food shortages, the U.S. Government still must subsidize a large portion of our agricultural exports.

The lesson is clear; free trade doesn't exist in the world, and never has.

Today all the world is in economic disorder. Industry in the Old World is depressed, and every European nation uses tariffs and other measures to protect their industry and domestic markets. And every one of them is depending upon exports to help them solve their economic problems. All are looking to America for help, because of America's generosity, and because the U.S. market is the largest and most lucrative in the world.

These are dangerous times for America, and we had better be aware of it.

Free trade for America leads in only one direction. It can only lead to less U.S. industry, and more unemployment and poverty. Its basic purpose is unmistakable. Ultimately it will bring U.S. wage and living standards down to world levels. Which it will surely do, if long continued.

By favoring free trade, the U.S. Government is making trouble for America. Free trade is basically an international share-the-wealth measure, designed for world betterment, but NOT to benefit America.

Estimates are that by the end of this century the mounting populations of Central and South America, and other Third World countries will swell the world labor force by more than a billion workers. Which will bring pressure on America to take more imports.

Another worrisome forecast is that by the year 2000 the U.S. will need 15 million new job openings to avoid serious unemployment. Some economists also predict that more depressions and recessions are coming to America. Some also predict that the American people will have to settle for a lower standard of living in the future, because of world competition.

Whatever is in the offing, my friend, America should be prepared. Imports that depress U.S. industry and prevent its full development, should be stopped. We should develop more of our country's magnificent resources and make the United States a more independent and self-sufficient nation.

America will never fully prosper if we depend on U.S. exports for our well-being. Foreign trade is unreliable trade. It's here today — and gone tomorrow. Right now U.S. foreign trade is 50 percent less than what it was just a few years ago. And it's mostly agricultural products and raw materials that comprise most of our exports.

ROUND THREE

Free Trade & Foreign Aid

W'HENEVER the foreign trade of the United States is discussed, the subject of *foreign aid* should also be considered, for the two are closely related.

For many years the United States has been lavish with its aid to other nations. All told, America has given the poorer nations of the world more than $130 *billion* in financial aid. The United States has also spent more than $2 *trillion* for the defense of Europe and to aid Japan. No other nation in history has ever been so generous.

Because of American generosity, many nations now rely on the U.S. for both aid and trade. Many have come to believe that America is rich and benign and open-handed, and quite ready to help them when they are in need.

Not long ago the leaders of 22 nations met in Cancun, Mexico to discuss Third World poverty. Prior to that time the United Nations had passed a resolution favoring a massive redistribution of wealth to Third World countries. The meeting in Mexico was to support that U.N. resolution. The suppliant countries wanted aid mostly to help them explore for oil and gas, and for industrial development. Presumably the financial assistance was to come from the wealthier nations of the world, but mostly from the United States.

In the past, officials in Washington had usually looked upon such requests for aid with sympathy, and had often responded with generous aid. This time, however, President Reagan said NO and advised them to go home and use their own resources for development purposes. Which was timely advice, and long overdue.

Most U.S. Government monies given to aid Third World countries have seldom served their claimed purpose. Most have been used by foreign nations to pay off their bank debts, and to enrich their politicians.

Proof is the fact that about 15 percent of those living in Third World countries own the wealth, and the other 85 percent live in abject poverty. Obviously, most of those countries need political and social reform far more than U.S. financial aid.

In 1981, the countries of the Third World owed the international banks the astronomical sum of $439 *billion,* up from $68 *billion* in 1971. Whether they will ever be able to pay their monstrous debts is doubtful. Only by getting financial aid from the U.S. Government and from other countries, and by earning money from exports, will they be able to pay their bills. If they can't raise the money in those ways, the international banks will be in real trouble.

Which explains, my friend, why U.S. foreign aid and trade are so closely related. And why both are so very important to some U.S. and international financial institutions.

Next look at the immense gains made by foreign industry in exports to the U.S. During the last 15 years, their exports to the U.S. have increased approximately 500 percent. The free-trade policy of the U.S. Government is mostly to blame.

Free trade has been very costly for America. It has caused a substantial loss of U.S. industry and employment. For when a people imports products their own industry could produce, their own industry and employment is lessened.

How could it be otherwise?

Without tariffs and import curbs, the United States will continue to be overrun with imports. In many instances, U.S. industry can't compete with imports. That's due to the lower wages and production costs in other countries. And also because foreign governments frequently subsidize exports. They give their exporters loans with easy pay-back provisions, and other emoluments. It's claimed that 30 percent of all export sales by Japan, France, and the United Kingdom receive government subsidies.

Worldwide, export subsidy payments are estimated at nearly $100 *billion* a year. By subsidizing their exports, foreign nations are able to sell more of their products abroad, and keep more of their workers employed. Also it helps them pay their debts.

Most damaging to U.S. industry and employment is the huge flood of products coming into the U.S. from Third World countries. South Korea is an example.

In South Korean textile and electronic industries, most workers earn less than 70 cents an hour, including housing and fringe benefits. 64-hour work weeks for labor are routine. The government sets most industrial and economic policy, controls credit, and operates all the banks. And South Korea's exports are booming, especially in machinery, textiles, and electronic products. One-third of their exports come to America, where they undercut U.S. products. And America's trade deficit today with South Korea is immense.

U.S. trade with Japan is another example of American trade liberality. Japan floods the U.S. with its products, yet has a long list of import restrictions and quotas that limit U.S. exports to Japan.

Another example is Western Europe and the European Common Market. The United States allows free entry for most products from those areas, even though Europe generally restricts U.S. imports.

It's been estimated by the U.S. General Accounting Office (GAO) that by 1990 forty percent of the steel used in America will be supplied by foreign mills. Another report from the same source, estimates that 65 percent of the footwear sold in the U.S. is now supplied by foreign industry, with the loss of 100,000 jobs in the U.S. shoe industry.

If U.S. industry is to develop, and American workers have plentiful employment, America's doors should be closed to imports that displace the products of U.S. industry. For a change, let us *Americans look after America,* and let the international financial and industrial corporations find other ways to make their profits.

ROUND FOUR

Imported Trouble

THE next few pages will show that every economic depression in U.S. history has come from foreign sources.

In the beginning, the British effort to control the economy of the Thirteen Colonies gave rise to the American Revolution and the birth of the United States.

United States ties with the Old World caused America's first major depression, the Panic of 1815. It was caused by the collapse of the English cotton market.

Next came the Panic of 1819, following the Napoleonic Wars. It was caused by the dumping of large quantities of English and European goods on the American market. Which badly damaged young U.S. industry, and the budding New England textile industry.

After that came the Panic of 1839, caused by the crash of the Liverpool cotton market, brought on in turn by famine in India. (All during those early years cotton was king in America, and whenever the world cotton market was depressed, economic conditions in America were also affected.)

In 1893 came the McKinley Panic, which was, up to then, more devastating than any other. It, too, was caused by the dumping of huge quantities of English and Continental European products on the U.S. market. That depression was ended when Congress established stiff tariffs to prevent continued excessive imports.

After those tariffs were established, America prospered for the next 35 years as never before. New industries were established all over America and new cities and communities grew around them. For the first time, the United States had the opportunity to develop its own industry and resources without being hampered by ruinous foreign imports.

Some historians have portrayed that period of American industrial growth as "The Golden Age of America."

Then came the most serious and damaging of all U.S. depressions. It was the Great Depression, which started in 1929. Despite many wild claims, the Great Depression was not caused by either Herbert Hoover or the Smoot-Hawley tariffs.

Plainly the records show that Depression, starting in 1929, was caused by worldwide depression, and the tremendous fever of speculation before then, fueled by foreign money in the U.S. stock market.

Before then, Europe had been in social turmoil, so European funds had been transferred to America for safekeeping. And those funds were either deposited in U.S. banks or invested in the U.S. stock market. At the time, no adequate system for regulating the U.S. financial system had been set up by the U.S. Government.

What made conditions so dangerous was that the foreign monies in U.S. banks were not long-term bank deposits. Most were short-term deposits. Also the U.S. securities held by foreign investors could be quickly liquidated at any time. And if both of those supports were suddenly removed from the U.S. financial structure, America would be in real trouble.

And that is exactly what happened. In 1929-30 Europe suddenly liquidated large blocks of U.S. securities. At the same time billions of dollars in foreign funds were withdrawn from U.S. banks.

Then the panic started. U.S. security prices tumbled. Billions of dollars in U.S. investment values were suddenly wiped out. Thousands of large and small American investors lost their life savings. Banks and investment firms saw their holdings and collateral shrink in value. Banks frantically called in loans for payment. Hundreds of banks closed for lack of ready funds to cover withdrawals. The entire financial system of America suffered near collapse.

Business and industry all over America shared in the disaster. Factories closed their doors and unemployment developed everywhere. Long bread lines formed in many towns and cities across America. Those were hard and anxious times, the likes of which should never be allowed to happen again in America.

The American people should learn something from the Great Depression, as well as from other U.S. recessions and depressions. We should see that while we have political and religious freedom, our great nation still lacks complete *economic independence.* For too long, America has been a partial ward of the Old World. And it's time now that we remove those shackles for our own good.

The United States can't be isolated from the rest of the world. But surely America can have more *economic independence.* We need to develop more industry in the United States, and more employment. We need to become a more self-sufficient nation. Which is the only way the U.S. will gain economic stability and solid growth, and provide better lives for the American people.

ROUND FIVE

Brainwashed America

B ECAUSE of propaganda, it's difficult to know the real truth about U.S. free-trade. Foreign governments, foreign industry, and the international banks all have had a hand in the effort to secure public support for liberal U.S. foreign trade policy. Those forces have been joined by some of America's larger wholesale and retail dealers, that have profited handsomely from merchandise imports. No doubt, that influence is largely responsible for the present free-trade policy of the U.S. Government.

Look at these forces lined up to influence U.S. Government foreign trade policy:

In Washington, D.C. there are an estimated 100,000 foreign representatives. Included are approximately 140 foreign missions, supporting 6,000 diplomats and their families. Those missions employ about 11,000 administrative and technical people. There are also about 500 foreign news reporters based in Washington, D.C. that influence U.S. public opinion and Government policy.

With such pressure, is it any wonder that foreign interests have been able to manipulate U.S. trade and aid policy?

In addition to those representatives of foreign governments based in Washington, D.C. there are scores of foreign agencies and trade associations established there for the same purpose. Here are some of them located in Washington, D.C.:

American Chinese Trade Council
American-Czechoslovak Chamber of Commerce
American Estonian Chamber of Commerce
American Hungarian Chamber of Commerce
American Japanese Trade Council
International Chamber of Commerce
Argentine-American Chamber of Commerce
Belgian Chamber of Commerce of the U.S.
Board of Trade for German-American Commerce, Inc.
The British Empire Chamber of Commerce of the U.S.

Chile-American Association
Columbia-American Chamber of Commerce
Ecuadorean-American Association, Inc.
French Chamber of Commerce of the U.S.
Foreign Commerce Club of N.Y. Inc.
Italian Chamber of Commerce
Japanese Trade Association
Lithuanian Chamber of Commerce
Mexican Chamber of Commerce of the U.S.
Netherlands Chamber of Commerce
Norwegian American Chamber of Commerce
Palestine Chamber of Commerce
Peruvian-American Association
Philippine-American Chamber of Commerce
Spanish-American Chamber of Commerce
Swedish Chamber of Commerce of the U.S.A.
Venezuelan Chamber of Commerce of the U.S.
The Netherlands Trade Commission
South African Reciprocal Trade Committee

Other associations and foreign trade groups that work to influence U.S. foreign trade policy are located in New York, Chicago, San Francisco, and other strategic locations.

Those listed here are based in New York City:

American Brazilian Association
American Importers of Japanese Textiles Inc.
The Asia Society
American-Turkish Society
Australian Trade Association
American Chamber of Commerce for Trade with
   Italy
British Trade Center
Brazilian Government Trade Bureau
Chamber of Commerce of Latin America
Cotton Importers Association
Dominican Chamber of Commerce of the
   U.S. Inc.
Far East-American Council of Commerce
   and Industry Inc.
Far East Conference
Finnish Chamber of Commerce of U.S.
Italian Chamber of Commerce in N.Y.
German-American Trade Promotion Office
Japanese Chamber of Commerce of N.Y.
Japan Export Trade Promotion Agency
National Foreign Trade Council
National Council of American Importers
   and Traders Inc.
Spanish-American Board of Trade
U.S.-German Chamber of Commerce

From the foregoing information you will see how much pressure foreign interests can apply on the U.S. Government to secure favors and trade concessions.

It's common practice in the U.S. Capital for foreign embassies and agencies to entertain influential members of Congress, government officials, and other important people connected with U.S. aid and trade. Bear in mind that it's no great problem for foreign governments and foreign interests to cultivate U.S. government people, or to propagandize the American people. There are no laws to stop them, and they have plenty of money available for that purpose.

Most propaganda has a selfish purpose. It also can come from many directions, and be disguised in devious ways. Very often it is deceptive, with its true purpose well hidden from the public. Here is an example of how faulty free-trade propaganda can be:

During the administration of President Lyndon Johnson, the U.S. Department of Interior asked for bids on two 600,000 kilowatt electric generators for the huge Grand Coulee hydroelectric power plant in Washington state. At the time there was considerable publicity that favored giving Russia a chance to bid on those generators. Some Government officials even favored it, claiming that it would (quote) "stimulate East-West trade."

Those who favored giving foreign industry the right to build the generators gave no thought to the fact that if foreign industry got the job, American labor wouldn't have the work, although they would have to share in their cost, as taxpayers. Nor was thought given to the possibility of trouble if Russia built the generators and replacement parts were needed later.

During that time, the news media was filled with stories and editorials favoring unrestrictive bidding. Most of the propaganda had the same theme (quote) *"If foreign manufacturers can supply comparable equipment at lower cost, why should the American taxpayer pay more to keep higher cost U.S. industry alive?"*

Here is another sample of how subtle propaganda can be. Recently a full-page and expensive advertisement was run in a prominent national publication by a phantom committee named the *Emergency Committee for American Trade.* What most readers didn't know was that the ad's sponsors were all international banks and multinational corporations with huge foreign holdings.

The advertisement read as follows (quote):

"America as a nation should have a liberal foreign trade policy and should promote the free exchange of products between nations, so that all people will prosper and world living standards become more equal."

That's a noble objective, and one that most people will approve. Yet, it's propaganda, pure and simple. Few Americans want to see the American standard of living lowered to world levels. It would help the world business community, but certainly not America.

It's interesting to note that Karl Marx advocated free-trade. He endorsed free-trade because he believed that it would eventually *wreck the economies of all capitalist countries,* including the United States. He stated, (and it's in the record) that he (quote) "favored free trade between nations because it would hasten the social revolution."

After reading this far, my friend, let me give you a warning. If you believe in AMERICA FIRST and don't approve of free-trade for the United States, keep it to yourself. If you don't, you will probably be called an "isolationist" or a "red-neck American."

Take heart my friend if you are ever accused of being a Nationalist —

"The professed internationalist usually sneers at nationalism, at patriotism, and at what we call 'Americanism.' He bids us forswear our love of country in the name of love of the world at large. We nationalists answer that he has begun at the wrong end; we say that, as the world now is, it is only the man who ardently loves his country first who in actual practice can help any other country at all."

THEODORE ROOSEVELT

ROUND SIX

Made in Japan

Hon has Japan, within a period of little
over 100 years, managed to emerge from virtual
isolation to become one of the three most important industrial and exporting nations in the world?

To start with, you should understand that the
Japanese are a highly skilled, dedicated, and fan-
tastically industrious people. Japan is also a closed,
homogeneous society. More than 99 percent of its
population is of pure Japanese ancestry.

The Japanese people are loyal and supportive of their government, of Japanese institutions, and of the industry of their country. Relations between Japanese labor and industry are more amiable than in the United States, undoubtedly because of the lifetime system of employment in so much Japanese industry.

That system *wouldn't do for America,* but it has worked well for the Japanese. It has made for more peaceful Japanese labor/industry relations. It has helped make Japanese labor more competent. And it's partially responsible, no doubt, for the productivity and efficiency of Japanese labor and industry.

Japan's rise to world trade and industrial leadership began after Japan's defeat by the United States in World War II. The war left Japanese industry devastated, and Japan in almost helpless condition.

During the 80 months of U.S. occupation of Japan under General Douglas MacArthur, Japan had severe inflation and even a shortage of food. It was then that the U.S. government organized the American Famine Emergency Committee and supplied nearly 900,000 tons of relief food for the Japanese people. That relief food is said to have saved 11 million Japanese from starvation.

Japan has had other serious handicaps that could have prevented its rapid trade and industrial development. Before Commodore Perry's voyages to Japan in 1853 and 1854, the Japanese had lived pretty much according to their ancient customs and traditions, and had existed in near isolation from the rest of the world. At that time Japan was hostile towards America and Western civilization. It was a virtually unknown country, without sizeable commerce or interchange with other nations.

Another disadvantage is that Japan occupies a small land area, a rocky archipelago of four small islands, altogether no larger than the state of Montana. Yet Japan supports 126 million people, approximately half the population of the United States on that small land area.

Another handicap is that Japan has few natural resources.

Probably no other nation, with so many handicaps, has ever accomplished so much trade and industrial growth in such a short time.

What are the reasons for Japan's remarkable progress?

One reason is that the Japanese government and Japanese trade and industry work together in directing the economic life of Japan. In that endeavor they have the full support of the Japanese people, who are extremely loyal to their own, to Japanese industry, and to their government. With that kind of unity Japan's progress was inevitable.

Just six companies control most of the industry and export trade of Japan. Those giant combinations of trade and industry are: Mitsui, Mitsubishi, Otoh, Marubeni, Sumitomo Sheji, and Missho-Iwai. Hundreds of smaller Japanese industries and commercial companies are controlled by those six huge cartels, and all six work closely with the Japanese government. All six also have close working relations with the Bank of Japan, which is government-owned.

Those lesser companies affiliated with Japan's Big Six organizations receive many benefits from their affiliations. For one, many are permitted to operate at small profit margins, often as low as one or two percent. With Japanese industry, a profit margin of three percent is considered reasonable. And in export trade, small profit margins are extremely useful to obtain marketing advantage.

Often Japanese industry has even been known to sell its products in the United States at below cost to secure market position. The Japanese usually aim for volume sales, and for long-term benefit, not quick profits.

Of the Big Six companies that control so much of the commerce of Japan, Mitsui is the largest. Nearly 2,000 lesser companies make up the Mitsui group.

The Mitsui group of companies includes: shipbuilding, aluminum, steel, chemicals, textiles, apparel, and innumerable other products. The companies affiliated with Mitsui all work together and cooperate in trade and financial matters. Mitsui also provides its affiliates with trade, technical, and financial support.

Japan's efforts to develop its industry and exports seemingly have no limits. Often the Japanese government will subsidize exports with low interest loans, special allowances, tax rebates, and other forms of assistance. Japan must export to survive and has structured its industrial and economic system accordingly.

Among those Japanese industries receiving a great amount of government help is the Japanese tool industry. Machine tools are a very important Japanese product, especially for export. The government works closely with the Japanese Machine Tool Export Association, and often helps set up export prices and regulates tool production.

America is a BIG market for the Japanese tool industry. Presently about 50 percent of the numerically controlled lathe and machine tools used in the United States are Japanese-made.

Towards Japanese trade and industry the Japanese government is both protective and benevolent. It protects its domestic market with tariffs. It has control over exports. It has bureaus that work closely with shipbuilding, computer, steel, industrial machinery, petro-chemical, and other industries of Japan.

Government bureaus also have considerable control over the investments and international transactions of Japanese industry. They can even set limits on the production of certain Japanese products. They also have frequently aided in the formation of Japanese export cartels.

The government of Japan is extremely competent, and keeps its expense at a minimum. It also spends less than five percent of its budget on Japanese military. Although Japan has a population of 126 million and is one of the world's richest nations, the United States keeps 45,000 troops in Japan for Japan's protection. Because of its savings in military expense, Japan is able to spend more for civic improvements, social investment, and the development of its industry and export trade.

The computer industry is an example of the generous aid given Japanese industry by the government. In the '70's that aid amounted to $225 million. Now it has a new ten-year program for computer development, estimated to cost more than $1 *billion.* Japan is determined to develop its semiconductor, computer and communications industries at any cost. Japan seeks world leadership in that field, and may well succeed.

In their struggle for first position in the computer industry, the Japanese have made numerous buyouts of U.S. computer companies. They have even engaged in industrial espionage to learn some of the trade and production secrets of their American rivals. (Which is no secret, but a documented fact.)

The Japanese have another effective device for securing export advantage. The government has grossly undervalued the yen, which serves to reduce Japanese export prices. Even the Japanese admit that their exports would be much less if their yen were not devalued.

Japanese industry has often been tongue-lashed for "dumping" its products in the United States at prices below those charged in Japan, or even below their actual production costs. Those "dumping" charges have often been made by U.S. industry and the U.S. government. Japanese industry has been accused and found guilty of dumping motorcycles, radios, TV sets, typewriters, hand tools, microwave ovens, computers, electric motors, steel plate, tableware, and even zippers in the United States. The United States has anti-dumping laws with severe penalties to prevent such trade infractions, but seldom have those laws been fully enforced.

Here are some of the products America imports in large quantities from Japan: automobiles, motorcycles, sporting equipment, golf clubs, pottery, glass, machine and hand tools, office copying machines, calculators, computers, TV sets, radios, stereo systems, tape recorders, textiles, clothing, watches, ball bearings, sewing machines, motors, typewriters, cameras, pianos, and even barber chairs.

There are few products that the Japanese will not make for export to the United States, if sales are promising. Because most of the products Japan exports to the United States are copies or adaptations of American products, their costs are less than American costs because they save the initial expense of product development, design, and market promotion.

In 1982, latest figures, Japanese industry held 25 to 90 percent of the U.S. market for electronic cash registers, watches, recording equipment, TV's, cameras, motorcycles, automobiles, and a long list of other products.

The marketing strategy of the Japanese is to concentrate their export efforts on products that promise large volume sales. They will also frequently sell their products at break-even prices, or even at a loss, to secure immediate sales volume and market advantage. Which explains why the Japanese give special export attention to automobiles, electronic equipment, tools, calculators, and other big-ticket products. Such products bring in large revenue, and also provide larger employment for Japanese labor.

No doubt the Japanese would like best to control the U.S. automobile industry. Since the oil crunch, they have been actively promoting the sale of their automobiles in the United States, and for 1984 have a U.S. sales quota of 1.85 million passenger cars. They have also set up subsidiary plants in the United States for the assembly of their vehicles, *using parts made mostly in Japan.*

Because of free trade, the U.S. market is the easiest for the Japanese to exploit. It is also the largest and most lucrative market in the world for Japanese products.

Next time someone tells you that U.S./Japanese trade is of utmost importance to America, remember these facts: from 1977 to 1983 the United States imported more than $100 billion in manufactured and industrial goods from Japan. And during that time, hundreds of U.S. industries were closed or without work, and many thousands of American workers lost their jobs because of it.

How about U.S. exports to Japan?

Most U.S. exports to Japan are grain, foodstuffs, and raw materials. Japan buys very few factory or finished products from the United States. On the other hand, Japanese exports to the United States are mostly finished products, requiring considerable labor to make. So, in our two-way trade with Japan, the United States loses employment, and the Japanese keep more of the *work* for themselves. The Japanese are smart people!

How about Japanese investments in the United States and the industries they have located here? Those are important to the U.S., of course, but you should know that those industries are mostly *assembly operations,* with parts manufactured in Japan and shipped to the U.S. for assembly. That way the Japanese keep most of the work and employment in Japan.

To aid U.S. industry and employment, excessive U.S. imports from Japan should be stopped. The Japanese don't allow imports in large volume to come into their country and we shouldn't allow Japanese imports in excessive quantity to come into ours.

U.S. industry just can't compete with Japanese or foreign imports "dumped" in the United States at cut prices. Neither can U.S. industry often compete with imports that are supported by foreign government subsidies. And certainly U.S. industry should not have to compete in the U.S. domestic market with imports marketed by foreign cartels and monopolies.

U.S. industry can compete successfully with Japanese or other foreign industry, if conditions are equal, and all compete fairly under the same rules.

The Japanese are an amiable and polite people and make every effort to win the friendship and goodwill of America. But don't let those pleasantries warp your judgment. The truth is that the Japanese are ruthless competitors, and have caused great damage to U.S. industry and employment. Don't be mesmerized into believing otherwise.

ROUND SEVEN

Lost Resources

THE story that follows is true. It mostly is about the fishing industry of Alaska. It is included here to show how industry and nations, like people, often covet the property and resources of others.

At one time the fisheries of the United States were one of America's greatest resources. But now much of that rich resource is gone. Over-fishing is largely responsible.

Today foreign fishing companies supply most of the edible fish consumed in the U.S. And strangely enough, most of that imported fish is caught by foreign fishing vessels, owned or subsidized by foreign governments, and operating in American offshore waters. America's one-boat fishermen have a tough time meeting that kind of competition.

The decline of the New England fishing industry clearly shows how foreign encroachment can wreck a U.S. industry. At one time, large quantities of cod, haddock, and other species of bottom fish were caught off Cape Cod and the Georges bank. That resource has since been over-fished. As a result, there are now 50 percent fewer New England fishermen in the industry than there were at its peak, and unemployment is high in the area.

Alaska's fisheries have also been badly treated by foreign fishing interests, mostly Japanese.

After World War II, Russia curtailed Japanese fishing in Russian territorial waters. So the Japanese moved their huge fishing operations into Alaska offshore waters, and into the Bering Sea.

When the Japanese first entered Alaskan fishing territory, they claimed they wanted only the abundant bottom fish in those waters. However, when they began fishing in Bristol Bay, which is the world's largest source of red sockeye salmon, it was a different story. They came into Bristol Bay with huge fleets of factory ships, trawlers and catcher boats. They spread their nets for 200 miles, often directly in the migratory lanes of salmon coming into the Bay for spawning.

Bristol Bay is an inlet off the Bering Sea. Most of the streams entering the Bay connect with interior freshwater lakes where salmon have spawned for generations.

When the Japanese set their nets to intercept the salmon headed for their natural spawning areas, they destroyed future Bristol Bay salmon runs. At the time Japanese fishing companies refused to heed even the most elementary rules for fish conservation. They were in Alaskan waters to net all the salmon they could get, regardless of the future of that great Alaskan resource.

Improbable as it might seem, because of the lack of government help, American fishermen in Bristol Bay threatened armed confrontation with the Japanese. Guns and ammunition were sent privately from Seattle to Bristol Bay for their use. (All this is a matter of record and is something many Alaskan fishermen will not forget.)

To give some idea of the size of the Japanese fishing operation in Alaska, here are some of the dimensions:

During one year, 1958, the Japanese had 14 fleets, including 356 catcher boats with 13,000 men, fishing in Alaskan waters. Some of their huge factory ships employed 500 workers, and were larger than many of Alaska's shore-based canneries and fish processing plants. Some of the Japanese trawlers were 300 feet long. Some used nets three miles in length, which is illegal for American fishermen. The Japanese objective was to sweep up all the fish possible, regardless of the hurt to Alaska and its resources.

To understand the Alaska salmon industry you should know something about *salmon,* their spawning habits and life cycle.

Bristol Bay salmon will swim hundreds of miles from their habitat in the Bering Sea to reach the interior freshwater lakes above Bristol Bay to spawn. They always return to the same lakes and gravel beds where they were born. After spawning, they die. Fingerlings develop from the eggs and when they reach sufficient size swim downstream to the Bering Sea. After two years living in the Bering Sea for pink salmon, and five years for red (sockeye) salmon, they then swim back to the same inland spawning areas from whence they came. Their arrival in these spawning grounds can be predicted almost to the day.

Mostly due to Japanese over-fishing, with resultant injury to Bristol Bay salmon resources, Governor Walter Egan of Alaska in 1974 declared Bristol Bay an economic disaster area and ordered it completely closed to commercial fishing. He blamed the Japanese (quote) "for the almost total destruction of the Bristol Bay salmon run." He also said, "The Japanese are fully aware of the damage they are doing."

About the same story holds for the halibut resources of Alaska and the North Pacific. In 1973, Senator Ted Stevens, of Alaska, protested Japanese over-fishing for halibut in Alaskan waters. At the same time the International Pacific Halibut Commission urged that international measures be taken to curb Japanese over-fishing for halibut in the North Pacific.

Better late than never. In 1974 the U.S. Congress passed the U.S. Fisheries and Management Act. That law established a U.S. 200-mile offshore fishing zone around both the Atlantic and Pacific coasts. In those corridors no foreign fishing companies are allowed to fish for salmon. They are, however, allowed to fish for certain kinds of bottom fish, under the supervision of regional fishery management councils.

This needed protection of the fishery resources of the United States has brought some new hope and optimism to the long-dormant New England fishing industry. New fishing boats have been built, and the State of Maine has helped finance the construction of new commercial fish piers, additional boat storage, and new facilities for the unloading, processing, and storage of fish.

For Alaska, it's a different story. Since the U.S. Fisheries and Management Act, the Japanese have made big investments in 27 of Alaska's largest fishing companies. They have now gained at least partial control over much of the fishing industry in Alaska and the Pacific Northwest. Those investments are owned by Mitsui, Itoh, Marubeni and Mitsubishi, all part of the Big Six combine that controls much of Japan's industry.

U.S. industry, be it fishing or other, should be protected from foreign commercial interests and nations that would acquire American resources for their own profit and benefit. As long as America remains an independent nation we had better keep watch over our U.S. resources and see that they are not seized and controlled by foreign commercial interests. Other nations follow that practice and the U.S. should do likewise.

ROUND EIGHT

We Forsake Our Own

ASK yourself this question: Should Americans buy the products of foreign industry when there are nearly *ten million* workers without jobs in America?

Is it good that U.S. wholesale and retail stores are loaded with foreign made clothing, textiles, shoes and thousands of other products? Most of which could and should be made in America.

Is it good that excessive imports have changed the occupations and lifestyle of thousands of Americans?

Now more Americans are employed in offices, restaurants, service stations, and in white-collar jobs. Service jobs do provide service, but of what lasting value are they?

I ask you: how long can we continue to enjoy a high standard of living in America if we have to depend on service jobs for our livelihood?

These are accurate figures: In 1983 there were *3 million* fewer industrial jobs in the United States than there were four years before. Right now industrial production in the United States accounts for only 23 percent of the U.S. gross national product, and employs only 19 percent of America's civilian labor force. Doesn't that tell you something?

Consider these examples of how foreign imports have affected U.S. industry and employment:

There are approximately 1,300 shops in the U.S. making machine tools. In 1980 they employed 110,200 workers. Just 2 years later, in 1982, they employed only 68,000 workers. But during 1982 the U.S. imported foreign-made machine tools valued at $533 million.

Then look at the U.S. tire industry. Foreign automobiles imported by the U.S. account for a loss of at least 10 million tires for the U.S. tire industry per year. Also spare tires are coming into the U.S. from Korea and elsewhere. Because of this lost business, Firestone and other U.S. tire makers have closed many of their plants, idling thousands of workers.

More than 50 percent of the iron and steel bolts, nuts and screws used in the U.S. are now imported. Most come from Japan, Taiwan, and India. Production and employment in that U.S. industry have been cut as much as 50 percent because of imports.

America has always been a leader in the manufacture of ball and roller bearings. But now the Japanese have entered the U.S. market, and by shaving prices have captured an important segment of the U.S. domestic market.

The U.S. petrochemical industry produces polyethylene and plastics, and has been a progressive and growing business. But now imports from Mexico, Asia, and the Middle East have slowed that U.S. industry.

The Japanese haven't been backward in selling their cameras in America. In 1982, they exported 3.6 million cameras to the United States. Now they are also promoting Fuji camera film in the U.S. (Which we don't need, as American-made film is good and is reasonably priced.)

TV's were first developed and made in America. At one time millions of sets were manufactured in the United States. Now most of that U.S. industry is gone. It has moved to Japan, Korea, Taiwan, and Singapore, where manufacturing costs are cheaper than in America. In 1982, the U.S. purchased foreign-made color television sets valued at $533 million.

Honda, Yamaha, Kawasaki, and Suzuki now make 90 percent of the motorcycles sold in the United States. In 1982, 780,000 Japanese motorcycles were exported to the U.S. If they had been made in America, think of the extra jobs they would have provided U.S. workers.

Microwave ovens were first made in the U.S. The Japanese simply copied the American product and exported theirs to the U.S. at cut prices. In 1979, they exported 740,000 microwave ovens to the United States.

In the early '70's, the manufacture of typewriters was a large and thriving U.S. industry. Now most of that U.S. industry is gone. Most typewriters now sold in the United States come from Japan. In 1981, the U.S. imported 603,000 electric portables alone from foreign industry.

Most of the sporting goods now sold in the U.S. are imported. Which includes baseball and tennis equipment, and even some golf clubs. They come from Japan, Taiwan, and Hong Kong. (Good stiff U.S. tariffs would quickly solve that problem.)

The U.S. glass industry hasn't been spared import damage. Foreign glass is used in the windshields, headlights, and other glass parts of foreign automobiles. Foreign car imports have made a big dent in the market for U.S. glass.

The Singer Company first started making sewing machines in the United States. Now they make most of them in Brazil. Which doesn't stop them, however, from selling their product in the U.S.

At one time the making of pottery and dinnerware was a large and thriving U.S. industry. Then the U.S. Cooperative Potters Union had approximately 30,000 members. Today most of that U.S. industry is no more, and now we get our china and ceramic dinnerware from foreign makers.

In times gone by, 40 factories made watches and timepieces in the United States. Now most of the 60 million watches Americans buy every year come from Japan, Hong Kong, Taiwan, Switzerland, and the Virgin Islands.

Jewelry and silverware manufacture has long been an important Rhode Island industry. In good times it has employed as many as 35,000 workers. Now that fine U.S. industry is threatened by imports from Israel, Italy, and Hong Kong.

Briggs & Stratton Co., at Wauwatosa, Wisconsin, has long been a maker of small engines for lawnmowers, generators, and other equipment. They make a good product, but now Honda of Japan has come into the U.S. market, and seeks some of the customers Briggs & Stratton has developed over the years.

It's hard to believe, but at one time 44 factories made woolen gloves in the United States. They employed approximately 5,000 workers. Now most woolen gloves sold in the U.S. come from Japan and Hong Kong, and the U.S. industry employs less than 1,000 workers. (Imports can even hurt small U.S. industry.)

America is blessed with almost unlimited resources and is one of the few countries in the world that could become almost self-sufficient. And that is an advantage we have failed to develop.

ROUND NINE

At The Crossroads

FROM 1978 to 1983 the United States auto industry suffered immense losses. Chrysler came within an inch of bankruptcy. And Ford, General Motors, and American Motors all were hurt. Most of that trouble was caused by the worldwide oil shortage, which caused radical changes in the U.S. market for automobiles.

Before the oil crunch, the U.S. auto industry accounted for approximately 20 percent of the U.S. gross national product, and employed nearly *six million* workers, directly or indirectly. It had factories in 36 states and assembly plants in 74 U.S. locations.

Many of those U.S. auto plants are now closed. Others have curtailed production. As a consequence, there are now 25 percent fewer workers employed in the U.S. auto industry. Which has had a tremendous effect on business and employment in the United States.

Before the world oil trouble, most small-size automobiles were made and used in foreign countries, mainly in Europe and Japan. Fuel-saving automobiles were needed in those foreign countries because of high gasoline prices. Oil prices had always been cheap in the United States, so American car buyers were less interested in small compacts. For that reason the U.S. auto industry didn't build them.

Then came the worldwide oil scare, and gasoline prices skyrocketed in the United States. Small gas-saving automobiles suddenly were in demand. But the U.S. auto industry was caught empty-handed and couldn't supply them. Compounding the problem: it ordinarily takes at least two years to develop a new model automobile.

Never before had the foreign auto industry been offered such a golden opportunity to sell their cars in the United States. And it didn't waste any time in taking advantage of that opportunity.

That's how the Japanese were able to capture so much of the U.S. automobile and small truck market. And because of their added volume, the Japanese have become the world's largest builder of cars and trucks, a leadership which the United States formerly possessed.

To compete with the Japanese, the U.S. auto industry has had to make many changes. It has had to trim its payrolls, close many of its plants, and cut costs wherever possible. It is even buying some of its small cars and trucks in Japan, so as to hold on to many of its customers and dealers.

Ford, General Motors, and Chrysler have also bought into the Japanese auto industry. General Motors now has a 34.2 percent interest in Isuzu Motors. Ford has a 25 percent interest in the Toyo Kogyo Co., which makes the Ford Courier truck. Chrysler has a 15 percent interest in Mitsubishi Motors, which produces Colt subcompacts and RAM small trucks for Chrysler.

To cut costs, the U.S. auto industry is now buying many auto parts from foreign manufacturers. It has also established factories in Mexico, Brazil, and other countries, where labor is cheaper than in the United States. Which they have done to cut costs, and compete with foreign car imports.

Ford, General Motors, Chrysler, and American Motors now have plants in Mexico making engines. Those Mexican factories will make approximately 1.7 million engines in 1984, valued at nearly $500 million. Those engines are for export to the United States.

Why has the U.S. auto industry established factories in Mexico to make parts for U.S. automobiles? It's because the average wage in the Mexican auto industry is about one-seventh of what it is in Detroit.

The *automobile industry of the future* is viewed by some as a great industrial complex producing motor vehicles on a global basis. They believe that U.S. car manufacturers will buy their auto parts from many foreign sources and then put them together in America for the U.S. domestic market. They believe that a global auto industry is close at hand. They believe that soon just a few immense conglomerates will control the manufacture and marketing of world automobiles. Which would spell catastrophe for this great American industry, and fewer jobs for American workers.

Like it or not, there should be U.S. tariffs on imported passenger cars, trucks and auto parts. And to be fair to the U.S. auto industry, those tariffs should be based on the difference between foreign and U.S. wage levels, plus the amounts of the export subsidies and allowances granted to exporters by foreign governments. Plus the considerable discounts provided by foreign money devaluations. If afforded such protection, the U.S. automobile industry would not have to produce its automobiles and trucks outside the U.S. All would then be built here in America.

Don't Sell the U.S. Auto Industry Short!

N ext time somebody brags about that revolutionary five-cylinder, front-wheel, turbo-charged foreign car he's driving, tell him this: U.S. manufacturers offered five-cylinder engines back in 1906, front-wheel driven automobiles in 1930, and supercharged engines in 1934.

America was the first country to mass-produce gasoline automobiles for general use, the first to build a car that traveled more than two miles a minute, the first to offer fully automatic transmissions, and the first to employ standardized parts.

It pioneered bumpers, electric starters and horns, force-fed lubrication, power steering, four-wheel hydraulic brakes, back-up lamps, gasoline gauges, crank-type and electric windows, all-steel bodies, paints in a wide range of high-gloss colors, safety glass, air cleaners, air conditioners, gasoline and oil filters, easily changeable tires, independent front-wheel suspension, seatbelts, energy absorbing frames, even computers to control engine and vehicle functions.

When somebody says American automakers haven't been innovative, ask him who developed the Jeep, the station wagon, the first manned vehicle to traverse the moon, the

12-month warranty? Who really made the first automobile affordable and reliable?

It was the U.S. automotive industry.

It accounts for one-fifth of the country's gross national product and one-sixth of its employment. It transforms more than 20% of this nation's steel output, 60% of its synthetic rubber, 50% of its malleable iron, and 25% of its glass into the cars and trucks that America wants and needs. And it will have invested more than $70 billion by 1985 to give us automobiles that deliver unsurpassed performance, efficiency, and reliability. That ranks as the largest privately funded investment program in history, dwarfing the Alaskan pipeline and even the government's Apollo program.

America's top two corporate spenders on research and development last year were both automotive companies. Their combined R&D outlays approached $4 billion.

The industry is waging an uphill battle against the ravaging effects of high interest rates, a tangle of government regulations, foreign competition, high labor costs, and prices spouting at the pump. Rather than retreat, it's determined to march on.

ROUND TEN

Steel In Trouble

M ANY watchers of the U.S. steel industry have doubts about its future.

During the past few years it has suffered staggering losses. In one year alone, 1982, it took losses of nearly *four billion dollars.* In that same year Bethlehem Steel, U.S. Steel, Republic Steel, Inland Steel, Armco, and Jones & Laughlin reported losses from mill operations and closures of more than *three billion dollars.* Those losses would cripple or ruin any industry, no matter how large or affluent. Large losses cannot continue if the U.S. steel industry is to stay in business.

Foreign imports have taken, and continue to hold a high percentage of the U.S. domestic market for steel. Right now, 22 percent of the U.S. market for steel is supplied by foreign steel mills. Which doesn't include the immense tonnage of steel imported in foreign automobiles. Those imports have not only caused U.S. mills to curtail production but have also disrupted the U.S. steel prices.

When an industry as large and important as the American steel industry experiences hard times, all America is affected. And most injured are America's working people and their families. It's impossible to fully understand the terrible human injury caused by unemployment. The great amount of poverty, hardship, and human misery caused by hard times in the U.S. steel industry is beyond comprehension. It's a frightening situation that should never have been permitted.

In the Mahoning Valley in Ohio, always a thriving steel industrial area, some 50,000 steel workers in 1982 were without jobs. In Midland, Pennsylvania, the Colt steel mill has closed. It employed 4,300 workers. Armco has closed plants in Texas, Ohio, and Missouri, laying off 5,000 of its 18,000 workers. Bankruptcy has closed the Allan Wood Steel Co. mill at Conshohocken, Pennsylvania. It formerly employed 3,000 workers.

Bethlehem Steel has closed its huge mills at Lackawanna, New York, and Johnstown, Pennsylvania. National Steel has sold its big mills at Weirton, Virginia, to its employees to keep them operating.

U.S. Steel has closed 10 of its mills and portions of six others, releasing 13,000 of its workers. Kaiser has closed its steel mill and iron mines at Fontana, California. Three thousand workers lost their jobs from those closures.

Hard times in the U.S. steel industry have also affected other industries, especially *coal* and *iron mining* and *transportation.* The upper peninsula of Michigan, famed for its iron mining, is one of those areas affected. So is the Mesabi Range area of Minnesota, where much of America's iron ore is mined. Until recently, unemployment in that area was near 50 percent.

The recent staggering losses of the U.S. steel industry cannot be shrugged off with indifference. Too much is at stake to let this basic American industry be lost. The U.S. steel industry has had an important role in the building of America. Without it, the United States would be a crippled industrial power.

U.S. Steel to put
15,400 out of work

PITTSBURGH (AP) — U.S. Steel plans to close six of its money-losing domestic steel plants and to reduce operations at 24 other facilities, eliminating 15,400 jobs. The company also has broken off talks on an investment and steel-importing deal with Britain.

The six steel plants to be closed are Lorain-Cuyahoga, near Cleveland; Ambridge, Pa.; Johnstown, Pa.; Shiffler, in Lawrenceville, Pa.; Elmira, N.Y.; and Trenton, N.J., the company announced yesterday.

Other plants, including the South Works near Chicago, will be mostly shut down, the company said.

The company said the closings would eliminate the jobs of 4,590 active and 10,896 already laid-off employees in all U.S. Steel operations in 13 states.

Many of the shutdowns will be completed by April 1984, the company said.

Chairman David M. Roderick, speaking after the company board held its year-end meeting, said that "while the decision to suspend operations at the affected units are difficult for the employees and communities involved, they were unavoidable in light of global economic and market conditions in steel.

"We intend to serve only those markets that we can supply with quality product at profits necessary to maintain viable operations," he said.

Roderick also cited non-competitive labor costs as "an important factor" in the company's decisions.

U.S. Steel lost $487 million the first three quarters of this year. Last year, the worst in the industry since the Depression, U.S. Steel's steel segment reported an $852 million operating loss.

"This is a day of terrible news for a large number of our members," said Lynn Williams, acting president of the United Steelworkers union. "It means that the process of the deindustrialization of America continues on despite all the reports of recovery."

The company said that with the closings U.S. Steel was cutting back its steelmaking capacity from 31 million to 26 million tons a year.

Talks were broken off between U.S. Steel and the government-owned British Steel Corp. U.S. Steel wanted its competitor to invest in the Fairless Works near Philadelphia in exchange for a guaranteed market for 3 million tons per year of semi-finished steel slabs.

The discussions had ended so the two companies could pursue other options, he said. He said the deal was off for "purely economic reasons."

British and American labor leaders had vigorously opposed the plan as a threat to jobs in their countries.

In London, British Steel Chairman Robert Haslam said his company had been negotiating for a $156 million stake in the Fairless Works, adding: "Those who opposed this deal should not regard this as a victory."

The largest cutbacks were announced for the Gary Works in Gary, Ind., where 2,580 positions will be eliminated, and at the South Works in South Chicago, Ill., 3,100 jobs will be lost, Roderick said.

What about the *future* of the U.S. steel industry?

Additional steel capacity is now building all over the world. New steel mills, mostly government-owned or subsidized, are being constructed in South Korea, Taiwan, Argentina, Brazil, Mexico, and the Philippines. Estimates are that in less than 20 years Third World countries will be able to produce 200 million tons of steel annually. And most of that steel will be exported, much of it, presumably, to the United States.

The U.S. steel industry just can't compete with foreign steel, most of which is subsidized by foreign governments and produced by cheap labor. In Third World countries wages and production costs are only a fraction of what they are in the United States. For example, in South Korea, labor costs at the giant Pahang steel mill average about $1.80 an hour. That mill, constructed by the Japanese, is one of the most modern and efficient in the world.

Foreign steel makers have made the marketing of steel in the United States almost chaotic. Often they have "dumped" steel in the United States at prices below the cost of production. Most have done so to keep their workers employed. Which they are able to do because most foreign mills are either subsidized or government owned.

In 1982, the U.S Department of Commerce found that the government-owned British Steel Corporation had received subsidies amounting to more than 40 percent on structural and plate steel exported to the United States. It also found that French steel exports to the U.S. received government subsidies of from 20 to 30 percent.

The Commerce Department found that the Belgium government subsidy amounted to 20 to 21 percent. It found that the Italian subsidy amounted to 18 percent. It also found that 13 steel companies in the European Economic Community received government subsidies, some as much as 26 percent. It found that steel was dumped in the United States by West Germany, Belgium, France, Italy, Rumania, and the United Kingdom.

Early this year, 1984, the European Common Market threatened the United States with trade restrictions if the U.S. government further limited European steel exports to the United States. Is it any wonder that in free-trade America, our steel industry is in trouble?

Japan has been cited more than any other nation for trade infractions. In 1982, Mitsui & Co. was fined for violations of U.S. anti-dumping regulations. That same year, Mitsui was also charged by Colorado Fuel and Iron, Pueblo, Colorado, with conspiring to control the strand-wire, nail, and structural parts market in the western United States.

That same year, 1982, Babcock & Wilcox, Beaver Falls, Pennsylvania, charged the Japanese with selling steel pipe in the United States at less than fair value. National Steel also charged the Japanese with "dumping" galvanized and cold-rolled steel in the United States.

Lukens Steel, Coatesville, Pennsylvania, also accused the Japan Steel Works, Tokyo, with "dumping" stainless steel in the United States. And Kaiser Steel, Fontana, California, sued Mitsui & Co., charging that Mitsui trade practices had contributed to the failure of the Kaiser steel operation at Fontana.

Even some of the smaller U.S. steel mills on the Pacific Coast have protested Japanese trade practices. The U.S. Treasury Department, after investigating the complaint of the Gilmore Steel Corporation, Portland, Oregon, found that the Japanese had exported steel plate to the West Coast of the United States at 32 percent below production and shipping costs. Just last year, 1983, Isaacson Steel, after many years of operation, closed its mill in Seattle, Washington. It blamed Japanese imports for much of its problems. Isaacson at one time employed 1,200 workers.

What you have just read is well-established information, widely circulated in U.S. newspapers and news media.

Does it make sense for the United States to import foreign steel when America has the mills and capacity and labor to produce all the steel America can use? (That's a question the American people should ask themselves.)

ROUND ELEVEN

Textiles, Apparel and Shoes

A MERICAN industry cannot match the prices of the textile and apparel industries of Third World countries. That is why textiles and apparel from Third World countries have such large sales in the United States.

Visit any clothing store in your area and note the number of garments that bear foreign labels. At least two out of every five sweaters, blouses, shirts, dresses, and other articles of clothing are made by foreign industry and labor.

Those imports are purchased for resale by U.S. wholesalers, retailers, and chain stores because they cost less than American products. Which doesn't mean that U.S. apparel and textiles are overpriced. It simply shows the spread between American and Third World wage and production costs.

Most U.S. textile and apparel imports come from Taiwan, Hong Kong, South Korea, Sri Lanka, and China. The average wage in the South Korean apparel and textile industries is 63 cents an hour. In the Peoples Republic of China the average is 16 cents an hour. In Sri Lanka the average wage is 12 cents per hour.

The average wage in the U.S. apparel industry is $5.33 an hour. In the U.S. textile industry the average is $6.12 an hour. Neither of those American wage levels are excessive.

Should the U.S. textile and apparel industries be penalized because of the low wages in other countries? Surely they should not be discredited and deprived of U.S. sales because of our higher American standard of living and wage levels.

The U.S. textile and apparel industries are important to America. In 1983 the textile industry employed approximately 750,000 workers, and the U.S. apparel industry 1,183,000 workers. Surely such large employers of American labor are entitled to some protection from predatory imports.

Another good reason why the U.S. textile and apparel industries are so important to America is that they are labor-intensive industries. Both employ large numbers of unskilled workers and minorities. And today that kind of industrial employment is not too plentiful in America. We need more of it, for the unskilled will always be with us, and will need jobs.

Surely America cannot neglect that kind of labor.

At last count, the U.S. textile industry numbered nearly 5,000 companies. And there are about 15,000 firms in the apparel industry. Which further shows how important those industries are to America.

Unemployment is a serious problem in the U.S. apparel and textile industries. In 1983, according to latest count, unemployment in the apparel industry approximated 650,000 workers. And in the textile industry nearly 100,000 workers. *Today there are fewer workers employed in the U.S. apparel industry than there were 40 years ago, despite U.S. population growth. Doesn't that tell you something?*

Not long ago the Republic of Sri Lanka published an advertisement in the *Wall Street Journal*. It urged U.S. industry to locate in Sri Lanka. Several inducements were offered. One was a 100 percent tax exemption for up to 10 years. Another was government assistance for the training of workers. The advertisement stated that the average wage in Sri Lanka was $1 to $2 a day.

What about the future of the U.S. apparel and textile industries? For a certainty, both will continue to face serious trouble and more unemployment unless cheap imports from Third World countries and China are curtailed.

More and more foreign countries are expanding their textile and apparel industries, and expect to unload their increasing production in the United States. China has even stated it expects to finance its drive to modernize Chinese industry from exports to the United States.

The world today is seeing large industrial development in Third World countries, fueled by low wages and plentiful labor. China is also emerging as a major industrial power.

China is already a large producer of textiles and apparel. In 1983, China exported textiles, fabric and apparel to the United States valued at $857.6 million. Its textile industry now employs five million workers and has 12,000 spinning and weaving mills. It now grows more than three million tons of cotton a year, second only to the United States. It also produces more than one million tons of synthetic fiber a year. It is now the world's largest maker of cotton fabric.

Wages in the Chinese textile and apparel industries are unbelievably low. In China's No. 2 textile mill in Peking, the top wage is 19 cents an hour.

The big squeeze is on. Never before have America's foreign trade deficits been so large, and the effects are showing up in industrial America and in U.S. employment.

You have just read of the troubles of the U.S. textile and apparel industries. Next turn your attention to the decline of the American footwear industry.

In 1983, (latest figures) the United States imported 380 million pairs of nonrubber footwear. Those shoe imports were valued at $16 billion and came mostly from Taiwan, Brazil, and South Korea. Those imports supplied 65 percent of the U.S. domestic market for nonrubber footwear. U.S. industry furnished the balance, *only 35 percent.*

Way back in the '60's nearly 1,000 factories manufactured shoes in the United States. With supporting industry (leather and shoe findings) it employed nearly 300,000 workers. Now there are only 300 shoe manufacturers left in America, and they employ less than 100,000 workers. Imports are largely responsible.

This decline of the U.S. shoe industry is not the fault of the industry. The American shoe industry has always made good footwear, and wages in the industry have never been excessive. They now average only $5.65 an hour.

What has hurt the U.S. shoe industry is that wages and factory costs are much less in foreign countries than in America. In the Brazilian shoe industry the average wage is 75 cents an hour. In South Korea and Taiwan they average 85 to 90 cents an hour. And besides lower wages, the shoe industries of those countries all receive government export subsidies.

Obviously, without some protection, the U.S. shoe industry can't meet that kind of competition.

ROUND TWELVE

Why Import Lumber and Paper?

AMERICA is fabulously rich in natural resources. High among those assets are the immense forest resources of the western and southern sections of the U.S. They cover an area of 700 million acres, more land than in all of the United States east of the Mississippi River. No other country possesses such large and valuable timber resources.

Washington, Oregon, and California are 46 percent forested, and hold one-third of the softwood timber of the United States. Redwood, spruce, hemlock, Douglas, and true fir all grow here.

Elsewhere, particularly in the Southeast, there are large stands of trees especially suited for the manufacture of pulp and paper. Much of that valuable resource is still undeveloped.

With all of this great resource, the United States remains the largest importer of wood products in the world. Two-thirds of the newsprint we use is imported. Also, one-third of the softwood lumber we use. Surely, here is *great opportunity for new industry and employment.*

During one year, 1982, Canada exported 20 million metric tons of pulp and paper to the United States. During 1981 and 1982 Canadian mills exported 17 million metric tons of newsprint to the United States.

In 1981 Canada exported softwood lumber to the United States valued at two billion dollars.

For many years the Canadian newsprint monopoly has had a tight grip on the lucrative U.S. newsprint market. That market now amounts to six billion dollars a year. Back in 1942, Canadian newsprint sold for $50 a metric ton. Now the price is $535 a metric ton, which is far higher than it should be. (Canadian prices clearly show that the U.S. should produce its own newsprint.)

There is no credible reason why Canadian mills should supply the United States with paper and lumber. We have the resources and raw materials to produce those products here in America. Futhermore, the United States needs to develop its forest resources. Also the U.S. needs the additional industry and employment the lumber and paper industries could provide our people.

The Atlantic States comprise the largest single lumber market in the world. It is the lumber mills of British Columbia, Canada, that now supply most of the softwood lumber used in that part of the United States. Meanwhile the lumber mills in America's Pacific Northwest are depressed and inactive, and many are closed for lack of business.

Why have British Columbian lumber mills been able to sell so much softwood lumber in the eastern United States? One reason is that Canadian mills pay less for their raw logs than do U.S. mills. They buy their logs from the Canadian government, at prices less than for U.S. raw logs. Which could be considered a form of government subsidy.

Another advantage is that Canadian money is discounted, which serves to discount the price of Canadian lumber. Right now that discount amounts to approximately 20 percent.

Which brings up this question:

Does the United States dare to apply import charges on Canadian imports, to compensate for the differences between U.S. and Canadian market prices?

Competition should be fair and not weighted more on one side than the other. Canada is our friend, but Canada always looks after its own interests *first,* and the United States should do likewise.   Isn't that a fair statement?

The United States cannot have a healthy and flourishing lumber industry so long as it imports 50 percent of its lumber from Canada. The same is true for the U.S. pulp and paper industry. We cannot import *$8 billion* of that product every year from Canada without it having its effect on the U.S. pulp and paper industry.

America has all the timber resources needed to increase the U.S. lumber, pulp, and paper industries. In the South there are thousands of acres, not suitable for agriculture, where pine trees grow fast and in abundance for pulp and paper manufacture. In other areas of the United States, particularly in the Pacific Northwest, there are great stands of forest just waiting for development. If these were used, many new industries would develop to provide needed employment for American workers.

Largely because of Canadian competition, many Pacific Northwest lumber mills are closed. Others, to stay alive, have been exporting raw logs to the Orient. Many others are sawing cull logs, not suited for export. The lumber industry in the Pacific Northwest is truly in a bad way.

Wood chips are also being exported for use in Japanese pulp and paper mills. Which has caused a steep increase in the price of wood chips for Pacific Northwest pulp and paper mills, adding to their production costs.

Never should the United States export raw logs to Japan or any other country. Canada doesn't allow it, and neither should the United States. Our forests are too precious a resource to be ruthlessly cut and sent by the shipload to Japan. Someday we will need those trees to fill the building needs of America.

Sixty-five percent of America's timberlands are owned by the U.S. government, which means that most of the lumber and wood products for U.S. future use will have to come from our national forests. For that reason, some big changes in the U.S. Forest Service are imperative.

Every cent of revenue from the sale of timber from the national forests should be used for improving conditions in those forests, especially for replanting programs and increasing timber yields.

More money is also needed for better management and a larger work force. As of now, most of the revenue goes into the U.S. Treasury, and the U.S. Forest Service lives mostly on Congressional appropriations.

If the national forests are to be fully utilized, they should NOT be considered as simply a playground and scenic attraction, as advocated by some environmentalists. The national forests should be protected and cared for, but at the same time used to create more industry and employment.

ROUND THIRTEEN

Problems of Agriculture

AGRICULTURE· is America's largest and most important industry, and it is an industry we should be proud of.

American farmers produce 20 percent of all the grain in the world, nearly one billion tons a year. They employ about six million workers, far more than any other U.S. industry.

In addition, the American farming industry is the sole support of hundreds of U.S. rural communities. It spends more for supplies and machinery than any other industry. It cultivates and cares for 2.4 million acres of U.S. farmland, with a value of more than a trillion dollars. And it stands alone in its ability to grow agricultural crops at less cost than the farmers of any other country.

Yet despite its mammoth size and success, U.S. agriculture is having a rough time of it. It presently faces some almost impossible problems.

U.S. agricultural prices are largely determined by world market prices. Which means that the American farmer must sell his wheat, corn, cotton, and other basic farm products at approximately the same prices obtained by foreign growers. Those world prices often fluctuate wildly and often are below U.S. production costs.

Over-production is another serious U.S. agricultural problem. Surplus farm crops always depress market prices. Which not only reduces farm revenues, but also injures those communities and industries that rely upon agriculture for their income.

In early 1983, the U.S. government owned or held as loan collateral $18 billion in grain and dairy products. Wheat then in storage amounted to a record 1,869 million bushels. Besides surplus grain, the U.S. government also held 2.4 billion pounds of surplus cheese, butter and nonfat dry milk. In 1983, because of surplus farm crops, the U.S. Treasury provided farm crop support money amounting to $12 billion.

Imports are another major problem of the U.S. farming industry. *The United States should never import agricultural products that can be produced here in America.* Yet we do import such products. Which is hard to believe!

In California and Florida the citrus and vegetable growers are hurting from Mexican imports. Mexican growers, using cheap labor, are growing more and more fruit and vegetables for the U.S. market. They now supply nearly 50 percent of the "winter vegetables" sold in the United States. And should that condition continue for long, Mexican imports could easily wipe out most of the "winter vegetable" growing industry of California and Florida.

France and Italy now supply nearly a third of the common table wines sold in the United States. Both the Italian and French governments subsidize their wine exports to America. According to the American Grape Growers Alliance, U.S. grape growers are losing an estimated $700 million a year because of those imports. There are approximately 16,000 grape growers in the United States.

Imports have also prevented larger development of the California olive industry.

Maine is famous for its potatoes. But even that American product is being hurt by imports. Canadian growers are now supplying a major portion of the potatoes used in the eastern section of the United States. The Canadian government subsidizes those potato exports to the U.S.

Raisin exports, subsidized by the European Economic Community, threaten the California raisin industry. (That U.S. industry is more important than you might think.) The annual California raisin crop amounts to 300,000 tons.

Even such a lowly American product as the mushroom has been hurt by imports. It is a $300 million United States industry, and is being badly damaged by imports from Taiwan, China, and South Korea.

How many different agricultural products can be grown in America? Who knows? It's anybody's guess, but when you consider the wide range of climatic and soil conditions in America, there should be no limit to the variety of farm crops that can be grown in the U.S. No other country has such an advantage.

Some years ago, 18,000 acres of farmland in Oregon were used for growing flax. At the time there were 14 small flax mills operating in Oregon. Now they are all gone. Reason: linen can be produced cheaper in foreign countries than in America.

At one time the raising of sheep was a big U.S. industry. Forty years ago 50 million sheep were raised each year by American farmers. Now only 12 million are raised each year. Which is an enormous reduction, considering the big growth of the U.S. market since that time.

The United States is importing large amounts of beef, lamb, and other meat products from Australia, Mexico, Brazil, and New Zealand. In 1983, the U.S. imported 1.231 *billion* pounds of beef from Canada, New Zealand, and Australia.

Those imports have slowed the production of cattle and meat products in the United States. Which has also reduced the U.S. domestic market for feed grains, of which America has a huge surplus.

Sugar is another farm product which the United States should never import. In 1983 the United States imported 2.952 million tons of sugar from the Philippines and Latin America. If all the sugar consumed by Americans were produced in America, it's estimated that 1.5 million acres of U.S. farm land would be needed for the growing of sugar beets, and another two million acres for sugar cane.

U.S. agriculture has another ominous problem to be concerned about. Now Europe is buying less U.S. grain and cotton than it once did. Many of the countries in the European Economic Community are now increasing their production of grain and cotton. Some are growing for export.

France now exports wheat to China and Russia, on which French farmers receive a government subsidy of $82 a ton. Argentina also exports wheat at reduced prices. Brazil now has larger soybean acreage, and is subsidizing exports.

In Europe and elsewhere, more and more farm acreage is being developed. In 1982, Argentina increased its wheat acreage by 17 percent. Since 1974 Australia has increased its wheat acreage by 43 percent. Since 1978, Canada has increased its wheat acreage by 19 percent.

The loss of a goodly portion of the U.S. export market for grain and other basic agricultural crops is a real possibility.

Should the foreign market for U.S. farm products shrink, as it already has, many American farmers will have to turn to new and different crops. And there should be no agricultural products imported that would displace our own. From that development U.S. farmers could very well benefit.

ROUND FOURTEEN

Resources In Abundance

NEXT comes a brief resume of the potential oil reserves of the United States, followed by information about America's large mineral wealth.

Few Americans know of the immense undeveloped oil resources of the United States.

Recently a wildcat oil well was drilled in the Rocky Mountains near the Wyoming-Utah border. That one well revealed a field estimated to contain one billion barrels of oil. Never had that area produced a drop of oil before.

Many places in the United States favorable for oil development haven't even been touched. Some haven't even been explored. It is known, however, that the United States contains some 163 billion barrels of recoverable oil resources, just waiting for development.

California, after years of oil production, still has crude oil reserves estimated at 3.64 billion barrels.

The outer continental shelf of the United States is also known to contain large deposits of oil and gas. The U.S Geological Survey estimates that there are 40 billion barrels of oil and 81 trillion cubic feet of natural gas under those offshore waters.

One expert high in the oil industry has expressed the opinion that "there is as much crude oil and twice as much natural gas underground in the United States today as we have used during the last 120 years."

An immense supply of oil is also contained in the huge oil shale deposits in Colorado and Wyoming. As much as 600 billion barrels of recoverable oil are estimated to be in those deposits. Some day the United States will develop and make use of that tremendous resource.

Forty-four percent of the land area of the United States is still owned or controlled by the federal government. That land area totals 1.3 billion acres. It's estimated that two-thirds of America's undeveloped oil and gas resources are under those public lands. The most promising areas, where from 30 to 60 percent of the land is government-owned, are in Wyoming, California, New Mexico, Colorado, and Alaska.

Many authorities in the oil industry believe that Alaska contains the largest potential deposits of oil and gas in the world. Some believe that Alaska's untapped resources, if developed, could make the United States entirely *energy independent.*

Many believe that the oil buried beneath the North Slope of Alaska might even exceed the oil reserves of Saudi Arabia. The North Slope is a vast arctic plain covering thousands of square miles. Its oil and mineral resources are totally unknown, but are believed by many to be of tremendous size.

Naval Petroleum Reserve No. 4, covering 37 thousand square miles in northwestern Alaska, is a prime area for oil development. Most of that area hasn't even been explored.

Next, turn your attention to the mineral resources of America. They, too, are abundant, but largely undeveloped.

Strangely enough, the United States now imports more than 50 percent of 23 essential minerals required by U.S. industry. We now import more than 90 percent of the cobalt, manganese, chromium, and bauxite we use. These are vital in the production of steel, machine tools, and other metal products.

The United States imports 81 percent of its tin, 77 percent of its nickel, 62 percent of its zinc, 61 percent of its potash, 51 percent of its mercury, and 50 percent of its tungsten; even though we have large deposits of those minerals here in the United States.

The United States has a huge supply of low-grade manganese, which can be easily and cheaply refined by electrolysis. Also large deposits of vanadium are located in Montana, Wyoming, and New Mexico. Tin occurs in both Alaska and New Mexico.

In Western Texas, New Mexico, and Kansas lie vast deposits of potash. Both Utah and Colorado have large deposits of tungsten. Copper, lead, and zinc deposits abound in Montana, Idaho, Utah, and New Mexico.

In the West Panther Creek area of Idaho is the world's largest deposit of cobalt. The United States now gets 75 percent of its cobalt from Zambia and Zaire in Africa. Is it the cheap labor in Africa that makes African cobalt so attractive?

Under the offshore waters of America, along the Atlantic and Pacific coasts, lie fabulous deposits of nickel, cobalt, copper, and manganese nodules, laid down over the millennia. Those deposits are in American offshore waters and are American property. However, the United Nations claims that resource "belongs to all mankind." (It's hoped that the U.S. Government doesn't give that resource away for foreign development.)

In Alaska, the U.S. Borax Company is now developing a molybdenum deposit at Quartz Hill, near Ketchikan, which could be the world's largest molybdenum resource. When in full operation the mine will employ nearly a thousand workers.

Today the mining industry of the United States is in deep depression, the worst in 50 years. Many U.S. mines are now closed and thousands of American miners are without jobs. What other nation in the world would allow such a condition to exist, if it possessed the mineral resources we have here in America?

The United States needs a healthy mining industry. It's needed for national defense, and it's needed to make America a more prosperous and self-sufficient nation. But most of all, the United States needs an active mining industry so that there will be work for American miners and livelihood for them and their families.

ROUND FIFTEEN

New Life For America

THE next few pages will deal with the moral aspects of free trade. And how free trade has affected American life.

For five years, from 1979 to 1984, the United States has had a total merchandise trade deficit of nearly $100 *billion*. And those deficits are increasing. For the year 1984, it's predicted that the deficit will climb to more than $100 *billion*. (Which is for *just one year!)*

Just what do those deficits mean to America?

Most of America's excessive imports come from Taiwan, Korea, Hong Kong, China, the Philippines, Mexico, Brazil, and other Third World countries where labor and production costs are dirt cheap.

With competition from such low-wage foreign industry, how can U.S. industry, serving the U.S. domestic market, exist without tariff protection? You answer that one!

Free trade is a disaster for America. It has destroyed a large amount of U.S. factory industry, and has had a disastrous effect on the lives of many Americans. It has closed the doors of many factories and industries in worker neighborhoods and communities, leaving many of those areas depressed and in desperate condition.

Free trade has seriously damaged America in still another way. Many workers, because of closed industry and lost jobs, have become cynical about America, and the blessings that belong to the American people.

Many have lost their homes, their life savings, and the established lives they had earned for themselves over the years. And those injured Americans cannot be blamed for being bitter.

If you have ever been without a job, with a family to support; you will know of the fear, anguish, and hardship that comes with unemployment. Unemployment is a fearful condition, and when U.S. trade policy prevents U.S. industrial development and fosters unemployment; that is something few Americans will accept.

Most Americans are strong believers in the high ideals of America, but because of *U.S. free trade* many now have become skeptics. They see the products of foreign industry and labor flooding the U.S. marketplace. They see how those imports have destroyed American industry and caused unemployment for many thousands of U.S. workers. And they can't understand why such conditions are permitted.

Free trade is not for America. Instead, the United States should strive for more economic independence. It's time that we protect and encourage more U.S. domestic industry, and produce here in America more of the products we use. It's time for America to become more *self-sufficient*.

Those are great ambitions, and if accomplished, the American Eagle will fly free and strong again. Then America will gain new and larger industrial development and employment. And then there will be more progress and prosperity for all of us!